Copyright © 2023 Sharon Kraus.

All rights reserved. No part of this book may be reproduced, stored, or transmitted by any means—whether auditory, graphic, mechanical, or electronic—without written permission of both publisher and author, except in the case of brief excerpts used in critical articles and reviews. Unauthorized reproduction of any part of this work is illegal and is punishable by law.

ISBN: 979-8-89031-207-5 (sc)
ISBN: 979-8-89031-208-2 (hc)
ISBN: 979-8-89031-209-9 (e)

Because of the dynamic nature of the Internet, any web addresses or links contained in this book may have changed since publication and may no longer be valid. The views expressed in this work are solely those of the author and do not necessarily reflect the views of the publisher, and the publisher hereby disclaims any responsibility for them.

One Galleria Blvd., Suite 1900, Metairie, LA 70001
1-888-421-2397

Pony, Poems, & Pictures

There's Little Miss Cowgirl, in her favorite hat,
sitting on a fence rail beside a yellow cat.
She's watching the horses, wishing she could ride.
She knows she's not supposed to when her Mom isn't outside.
Little Miss Cowgirl is wondering right now,
if she should jump on her pony and go chase a cow.
She knows her mom is busy and won't be out for a while.
As these thoughts go through her head, little Miss begins to smile.

She's sure she can do this, her mom will never know.
She gets on her pony's back and to the pasture they go.
Little cowgirl throws a rope, tries to catch a calf.
She catches a small one. She's been gone an hour and a half.
Her mother has been calling her and looking all around.
She has a pretty good idea where the cowgirl can be found.
The mother of the Little Miss Cowgirl wants to be sure she's ok.
She finds her on her pony and scolds – "Don't you ever listen to what I say?"

Blue Ribbon Day

Getting ready for a horse show, there's work to be done.
A list of things to do before any ribbons can be won:

1. Catch the horses and give them a bath.
2. Brush manes and tails, trim their bridle path.
3. Put on show sheen and then hoof black.
4. Clean and load up all the show tack.
5. Get buckets for water and a bale of hay.
6. Pack shirts, hats and boots that we need for the day.

You can do this too, this is the way.
Some simple instructions for a Blue Ribbon Day!

A Boy and His Pony

Little boy on his pony, his mother watches him ride.
She likes the way he handles his horse. She smiles, beaming with pride.

He says he's, "gonna be a cowboy," for now her little buckaroo.
Always in cowboy boots, he won't wear a regular shoe.

Everyday he wears a western shirt and his Wrangler jeans.
He says he's going to be a cowboy as soon as he turns fifteen.

His favorite toy isn't a truck, it is his best trick rope,
and if he can't ride his horse, he'll sit around a mope.

Most summer days he packs a lunch in his saddlebags.
"Be careful, don't go far," she says. The boy says, "Oh mom, just nags."

She's on her flashy paint, the horse was jigging and prancing.
Sidestepping left and right, it looked like the two were dancing.

There they were, the two of them, handsome horse and pretty girl,
racing around the arena, dust flying around them in a whirl.

They were really fun to watch. The horse would jump and rear,
hooves reaching up to the sky as light and easy as running on air.

The girl and her horse together, they were a glorious sight.
Showing all the splendor of a horse's beauty and might.

Due Any Day

We've been waiting and watching for days on end.
Wondering what the good Lord would send.

Would it be a pretty filly or a handsome colt?
What would be the color of the foal's coat?

Finally the big day arrives. I stayed right here with her so I could see the wonderful miracle of birth!

The mare gets anxious. I tell her everything's ok.
She has a clean bed of straw and some fresh hay.

She starts pacing the barn and keeps turning around.
I climb from the hayloft, down to the ground.

The mare is up and down, and soon I can see,
the baby is born, she looks over at me.

Lacy nickers at her and licks off the sack.
The foal is a girl and she is solid black.

Sassy Sissy

Today she is an Indian girl, on her trusty steed.
She can ride him bareback, for a saddle there is no need.

She rides her pony to the lake, over by the cattails.
Down the hill, across a creek, all around the park trails.

She likes her little pony; he is her favorite buddy.
She rides him whenever she can, whether it's sunny of muddy.

They go on all these rides and have wonderful adventures.
"Be careful," her mother warns. "Oh I am," the little girl assures.

She's a sassy little girl, it's easy to see. I'm sure you can,
our little Indian girl, happy-go-lucky, Elisabeth Ann.

Chestnuts and Bays, Palominos and Greys

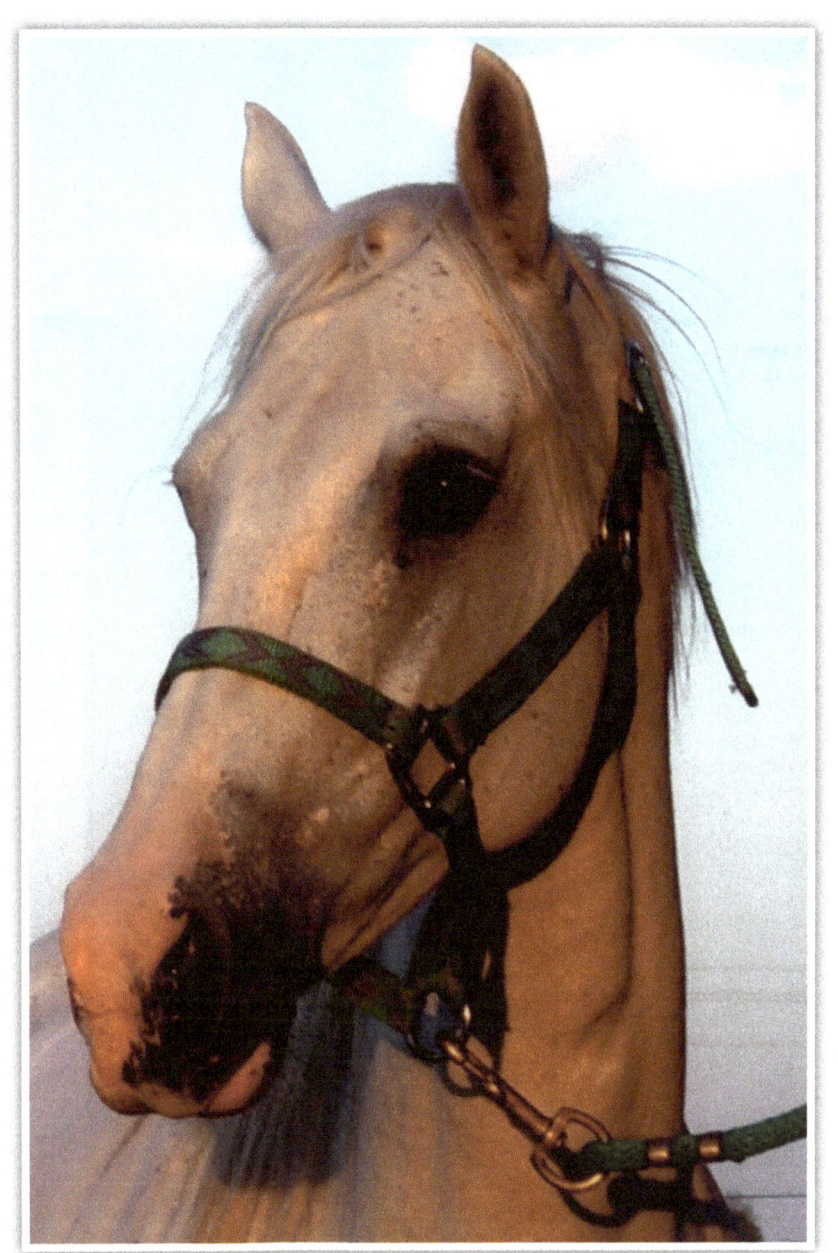

There's a strawberry roan in the field over there, and a Palomino with the gold colored hair.

That dapple grey is a beautiful horse.
But so is that black and white paint, of course.

So many decisions and choices, have I.
I can't keep them all, but I'd sure like to try!

The grey is the prettiest,
but the sorrel is fast.
The bay is a young horse,
so for years he would last.

The appaloosa is showy
with all her spots.
Kids always like horses
with polka dots.

To choose only one would
be a difficult task.
Do I have to go through
such torture, I ask.

The chestnut is a sweetheart, the buckskin is so tall.
I love the pinto, but she's most expensive of all.

All the pretty horses, but the one that I like best.
The one I think is special and stands out from the rest.

Has a personality that is just perfect.
Of all the horses, she's the one I want to get.

A Girl's Fascination with Horses

A girl's fascination starts at a very young age. All the parents keep hoping they will quickly get through this stage.

Usually if the begging doesn't stop, if it goes on for years and years, we break down and get a horse so there won't be anymore tears.

And on that special, happy day
when finally a horse is hers,
we won't regret our decision
the delighted girl assures.

She promises to be out in
the barn each morning,
each evening, too.
To take care of the horse and
all the chores she has to do.

I can tell that she is happy
there's a sparkle in her eyes.
She goes to the horse and
hugs him! A horse of my own
she sighs.

When I Ride My Horse

When I ride my horse, the
wind blows through my hair.
We race the wind, and we
don't have a care.

Up hills and down,
over creeks we fly.
Under a canopy of trees,
the hours go by.

We've been out here all day,
enjoying the sun.
Walking and trotting
then into a run.

When we get back home,
I give her a treat.
I brush her real good
and pick out her feet.

She runs out to the pasture,
the others all greet her.
With nickers and neighs,
they ask where we were.

She tells them about the deer
that we saw.
All the woodland animals.
And the trees standing tall.

She tells them about the soft,
warm breeze,
and the sun filtering down
between the leaves.

When they go back to eating
all their grain and hay,
all I can think is that it's been
a wonderful day.

Baling Hay

Baling hay in the summer heat. Get the bales stacked, tight and neat. The boys take turns picking up hay. They're rather drive the tractor all day. The guys joke around so the time goes fast. They make a good day out of working in grass. Fresh cut hay has such a sweet smell. Taking care of livestock suits me well.

Four Sisters

Four sisters riding together on their horse's back.
Hold on to the little one so she doesn't fall off Jack.

He's a good horse, all those girls he'll willingly pack.
He just plods along while the girls go on, yackity-yak.

If he gets lazy, the one in the back gives him a little smack.
It's a rough ride when he's trotting, he's not a Cadillac!

But if it's a ride you want, he'll take you piggy back.
When they're done, they go to the barn and remove his tack.
Then give him an apple and some oats for a special snack.

Coyote Trick Riders

Here they come, the Coyote Trick Riding Team!
Living the life of every girl's dream.

You can see them at rodeos, on summer day,
riding around the arena, all the smiles and waves.

Horses and girls looking polished and fine,
dressed up in sequins, they sparkle and shine.

Horses galloping fast, a cloud of dust in their trail.
Oh to live the life of a trick riding gal.

Maria and Katie, daredevil trick riders,
rodeo committees, their job provider.

Standing on the back of a galloping horse,
hanging upside down running through the course.

They go all summer from place to place,
rodeo entertainment in spandex and lace.

Just some cowgirls getting all dolled up.
Heading for a rodeo in a pickup truck.
Pack everything up, with horses in tow.
On their way across country to put on a show.
Seeing all the people, hearing the crowd cheer.
Having fun with friends, that's what brings them here.

They sign autographs and teach girls how to be,
Like the coyotes, riding horses, wild and free.

At Wild West shows, they had lots of fun.
In competitions the trickriding troupe won.

Twenty thousand miles in ninety days,
eight different states on an adventure that pays!

TACK ROOM

So here we have all this cowboy gear,
but keeping it clean is a pain in the rear.
Someone always wants to try something new,
and need equipment for the event that they do.

There's all the tack to harness the team.
Genny's saddle she won as Rodeo Queen.

There are bits, buckles and spurs with jingle bobs.
Taking care of everything is a full time job.

When you go inside a barn, this is what you find:
things for our horses, supplies of all kinds.

My brother, Brian, said I should go to his island, where life is slow.
"Come and stay here a while. It's guaranteed to make you smile."

A hundred acres and a log cabin on an island.
Riding horses on the beach does sound grand.

"No troubles here, you'll have no responsibility.
Two whole weeks of living fancy free."

"Things to do here, aren't too much, just long walks by the ocean and such."
Moonlit nights and the lure of the sea, all these visions began beckoning me.
"We have nice horses here to ride. You'll like riding on the beach in the tide."

The thought of swimming in water that's 80 degrees,
sand in my toes and a warm southern breeze.

On an island in the summer sun, was all sounding like a lot of fun.
Everything about it had so much appeal; I decided to make this fantasy real.

We found a place where could ride on the beach.
We talked to a lady and asked for a horse for each.

She said she had many nice horses to ride,
she said they were calm, but I think that she lied.

When we got them saddled and ready to go,
they were all excited and wouldn't walk slow.

They liked to run and play in the surf.
They wanted to be in the water, not on dry turf.

We walked through the ocean to a sand bar,
we all got wet going out there so far.

But it was a hot summer day and it felt good,
we would have stayed there all day if we could.

We had to get the horses in before high tide,
so we turned around for the rest of our ride.

On our way back, we let our horses run,
before we were ready, our time there was done.

PITCHFORKS and SHOVELS

Pitchforks and Shovels

When you have a horse, there's always work to do.
We can't go ride until the work is through.

I pick up horse pucky for hours on end,
cleaning the barn for my furry friend.

When it's all done and fresh straw is put down,
she comes inside and leaves a fresh mound.

It is never ending and the job seems thankless,
but it has to be done so I better clean this mess.

Barrel Race

Time for a barrel race! My horse is ready, I am, too.
As soon as they open the gate, we'll hurry on through.

My horse is ready to run, he's pawing and pacing,
ready to win at this game of barrel racing.

Jet knows what to do, if we make a good run.
In about sixteen seconds, we should be done.

Running around the arena with hooves barely touching the ground,
racing from one to the other, the barrels we go round.

It happens quickly but takes lots of practice.
There's not anything I'd rather do than this.

When my turn is over and I've cooled down my horse,
I go watch the others run through the course.

One after another, around the barrels they go.
It's exciting to see, they put on a good show!

With dirt flying around them, horses galloping by,
I bet everyone watching wants to give it a try.

You'll need a special horse, one that loves to run.
You really should try it, barrel racing is fun!

IOWA RODEO

That pretty girl is an Iowa Rodeo Association Queen.
When she was little, this was just a dream.

She would look up to the Queens and admire them so,
that one day she would be one, little did she know.

ASSOCIATION QUEEN

She was different than the others, not so many jewels and curls,
but an excellent horsewoman, they picked from all the girls.

She could ride, the girl and her horse, a glorious sight.
She had a good seat, her hands on the reins were light.

It looked like they were dancing, this horse and the pretty girl,
riding around the arena, dust flying around in a whirl.

After fashion shows, horsemanship and interviews,
"Miss Congeniality" was picked for Miss IRA 2002.

We were all so excited that she really won.
Her expectations were just to go have fun.

All the high dollar horses and saddles didn't win the prize,
it was love of rodeo they saw in her smile and twinkling eyes.

When she rides her paint horse on the rodeo grounds,
little girls admire the rodeo queen with her shiny crown.

She gives them rides on her horse she used to barrel race.
She leads them each around with a big smile on their face.

Vocabulary

Bit - the metal piece that fits in a horse's mouth

Bridle - the headgear a horse wears

Buckaroo - another name for a cowboy

Colt - a young male horse

Filly - a young female horse

Foal - a young horse, male or female

Grain - feed for horses

Hay - grass that has been mowed and dried

Mare - a female horse of a mature age

Pasture - land suitable for grazing animals

Pitchfork - a farm tool used for lifting hay

Tack - equipment used in horse activities

Trick riding - performing stunts on a galloping horse

About the Author

My name is Sharon. I raised six children and lots of animals. My family always had horses and ponies and had a lot of fun with them. These pictures and poems are of, and about some of our times with our ponies.

www.ingramcontent.com/pod-product-compliance
Lightning Source LLC
LaVergne TN
LVHW072128060526
838201LV00071B/4997

9798890312075